POWER
POSITIVITY

I AM
KIND

quadrille

THREE THINGS IN HUMAN LIFE ARE IMPORTANT.

THE FIRST IS TO BE KIND. THE SECOND IS TO BE KIND. AND THE THIRD IS TO BE KIND.

Henry James

**KINDNESS
IS WISDOM.**

Philip James Bailey

WE ARE RICH ONLY THROUGH WHAT WE GIVE ...

AND POOR ONLY THROUGH THROUGH WHAT WE REFUSE.

Anne Sophie Swetchine

NO KIND ACTION EVER STOPS WITH ITSELF. ONE KIND ACTION LEADS TO ANOTHER. GOOD EXAMPLE IS FOLLOWED. A SINGLE ACT OF KINDNESS THROWS OUT ROOTS IN ALL DIRECTIONS, AND THE ROOTS SPRING UP AND MAKE NEW TREES. THE GREATEST WORK THAT KINDNESS DOES TO OTHERS IS THAT IT MAKES THEM KIND THEMSELVES.

Amelia Earhart

LIFE IS MADE UP, NOT OF GREAT
SACRIFICES OR DUTIES, BUT
OF LITTLE THINGS, IN WHICH
SMILES AND KINDNESSES
AND SMALL OBLIGATIONS,
GIVEN HABITUALLY, ARE WHAT
WIN AND PRESERVE THE
HEART, AND SECURE COMFORT.

Humphrey Davy

BE KIND. EVERYONE YOU MEET IS CARRYING A HEAVY BURDEN.

Ian Maclaren

**FOR ATTRACTIVE LIPS,
SPEAK WORDS OF KINDNESS.
FOR LOVELY EYES, SEEK
OUT THE GOOD IN PEOPLE.**

Sam Levenson

PRACTICE RANDOM KINDNESS AND SENSELESS ACTS OF BEAUTY.

Anne Herbert

WHAT DO WE LIVE FOR, IF IT IS NOT TO MAKE LIFE LESS DIFFICULT FOR EACH OTHER?

George Eliot

BEING CONSIDERATE OF OTHERS WILL TAKE YOUR CHILDREN FURTHER IN LIFE THAN ANY COLLEGE DEGREE.

Marian Wright Edelman

A SMALL ACT OF KINDNESS COULD CHANGE SOMEONE'S LIFE.

Emma Bunton

YOU HAVE NOT LIVED A PERFECT DAY UNTIL YOU HAVE DONE SOMETHING FOR SOMEONE WHO CAN NEVER REPAY YOU.

I PREFER YOU TO MAKE
MISTAKES IN KINDNESS
THAN WORK MIRACLES
IN UNKINDNESS.

Mother Teresa

THE IDEALS THAT HAVE LIGHTED MY WAY, AND TIME AFTER TIME HAVE GIVEN ME NEW COURAGE TO FACE LIFE CHEERFULLY, HAVE BEEN KINDNESS, BEAUTY, AND TRUTH.

Albert Einstein

REMEMBER THERE'S NO SUCH THING AS A SMALL ACT OF KINDNESS. EVERY ACT CREATES A RIPPLE WITH NO LOGICAL END.

Scott Adams

A KINDNESS IS NEVER WASTED.

Aesop

ALWAYS LOOK CHEERFUL – THAT MAKES PEOPLE FEEL GOOD AND DOESN'T COST ANYTHING.

Catharina Elisabeth Goethe

A LITTLE KINDNESS GOES A LONG WAY.

**DON'T BE
YOURSELF –
BE SOMEONE
A LITTLE NICER.**

Mignon McLaughlin

I HAVE ALWAYS BELIEVED
KINDNESS HAS MANY FORMS.
SOME QUITE OBVIOUS, SOME
MORE SUBTLE. SOME ARE
AN EXACT SHAPE AND SOME
KINDNESS, I HAVE FOUND, IS
MORE REACHING, SURROUNDING,
LIKE AN EMBRACE.

Julia Roberts

ONE OF THE KINDEST THINGS
THAT ANYBODY'S EVER DONE
FOR ME IS ASKED ME HOW I AM
AND REALLY WANTED TO KNOW.
BECAUSE I THINK WHEN WE
ASK PEOPLE HOW THEY ARE,
WE'RE OFTEN NOT PREPARED
TO REALLY BE PRESENT FOR
AN HONEST ANSWER.

Kerry Washington

SHALL WE MAKE A NEW RULE OF LIFE FROM TONIGHT: ALWAYS TO TRY TO BE A LITTLE KINDER THAN IS NECESSARY?

J.M. Barrie

**KINDNESS CAN BE
A SUPERPOWER.
ALL WE CAN DO IS
LEAD BY EXAMPLE.**

Sarah Ferguson

WHAT IS THE QUALITY I MOST LIKE IN SOMEONE?

I WOULD SAY KINDNESS.

Zendaya

IT TAKES COURAGE TO BE KIND.

Maya Angelou

IT IS A LITTLE
EMBARRASSING THAT
AFTER FORTY-FIVE
YEARS OF RESEARCH
AND STUDY, THE BEST
ADVICE I CAN GIVE
PEOPLE IS TO BE A
LITTLE KINDER TO
EACH OTHER.

Aldous Huxley

NO SMALL ACT GOES
UNNOTICED. IT WILL
HELP YOUR OWN HEART,
MAYBE EVEN MORE
THAN THE RECIPIENTS.

Jennifer Oldham

SPEAK KINDLY TO YOURSELF. I THINK THE KINDER YOU ARE TO YOURSELF, THE KINDER YOU WILL BE FOR OTHER PEOPLE.

Sabrina Carpenter

WE ALWAYS HAVE TO
ERR ON THE SIDE OF
KINDNESS BECAUSE
YOU NEVER, EVER KNOW
WHAT SOMEBODY'S
CARRYING OR WHAT
THEY'RE GOING THROUGH.

Taraji P. Henson

GIVE OF YOURSELF, GIVE AS MUCH AS YOU CAN! AND YOU CAN ALWAYS, ALWAYS GIVE SOMETHING, EVEN IF IT IS ONLY KINDNESS!

Anne Frank

**TO EXTEND YOURSELF
IN KINDNESS TO ANYBODY
IS AN EXTENSION IN
KINDNESS IN THE WORLD.**

Oprah Winfrey

THROW KINDNESS AROUND LIKE CONFETTI.

Olivia Rodrigo

THERE ARE SO MANY WAYS TO
MISUNDERSTAND PEOPLE AND
TO FORGET THAT, AT THE END
OF THE DAY, YOUR NEIGHBOUR
IS VERY LIKELY TO GIVE YOU
THE SHIRT OFF THEIR OWN
BACK ... I JUST REMEMBER THAT
EVERYBODY I COME IN CONTACT
WITH IS SORT OF, IN THEIR
OWN WAY, HEROICALLY KIND.

Pedro Pascal

IN THE FACE OF ISOLATIONISM,
PROTECTIONISM, RACISM,
THE SIMPLE CONCEPT OF
LOOKING OUTWARDLY AND
BEYOND OURSELVES, OF
KINDNESS AND COLLECTIVISM,
MIGHT JUST BE AS GOOD
A STARTING POINT AS ANY.

Jacinda Ardern

TREAT PEOPLE WITH KINDNESS.

Harry Styles

KINDNESS AND PATIENCE ARE THE MOST IMPORTANT ATTRIBUTES IN LIFE.

Holly Willoughby

WHEREVER THERE IS A HUMAN BEING, THERE IS AN OPPORTUNITY FOR KINDNESS.

Seneca

I AM LEARNING THAT YOU CAN BE KIND AND BE STRONG.

Beyoncé

AS CUSTODIANS OF THE PLANET, IT IS OUR RESPONSIBILITY TO DEAL WITH ALL SPECIES WITH KINDNESS, LOVE, AND COMPASSION.

Richard Gere

BE KIND TO EVERY KIND, NOT JUST MANKIND.

Anthony D. Williams

KINDNESS IS UNCONQUERABLE.

Marcus Aurelius

KINDNESS IS FREE, YOU SHOULD SPRINKLE IT LIKE SUGAR, LIKE SPRINKLES.

Ariana De Bose

BE KIND TO YOURSELF. YOU'RE DOING THE BEST YOU CAN.

**KINDNESS
IS POWERFUL.**

PRACTICE KINDNESS ALL DAY TO EVERYBODY AND YOU WILL REALISE YOU'RE ALREADY IN HEAVEN NOW.

Jack Kerouac

KIND GESTURES HAVE TO BE SO WELL THOUGHT-OUT. YOU HAVE TO REALLY PUT YOURSELF IN OTHER PEOPLE'S SHOES TO KNOW WHERE THEY'RE AT AND TO REALLY BENEFIT THEM.

Jennifer Coolidge

DON'T EVER FORGET THAT YOU'RE
A CITIZEN OF THIS WORLD, AND
THERE ARE THINGS YOU CAN DO
TO LIFT THE HUMAN SPIRIT –
THINGS THAT ARE EASY, THINGS
THAT ARE FREE, THINGS THAT
YOU CAN DO EVERY DAY: CIVILITY,
RESPECT, KINDNESS, CHARACTER.

Aaron Sorkin

IF NATURE HAS MADE YOU FOR
A GIVER, YOUR HANDS ARE
BORN OPEN, AND SO IS YOUR
HEART; AND THOUGH THERE
MAY BE TIMES WHEN YOUR
HANDS ARE EMPTY, YOUR
HEART IS ALWAYS FULL.

Frances Hodgson Burnett

NOTHING CAN MAKE OUR LIFE, OR THE LIVES OF OTHER PEOPLE, MORE BEAUTIFUL THAN PERPETUAL KINDNESS.

Leo Tolstoy

KINDNESS,
KINDNESS,
KINDNESS.

Susan Sontag

I TRY TO PRACTICE BEING KIND ...

I 'TRY' IT, BECAUSE IT IS A PRACTICE.

Michelle Obama

LET US BE KIND.
LET US BE GENEROUS.
LET US BE FULL OF GRACE.
LET US SEE THE LIGHT
IN ALL YOUR PEOPLE
AND BE GUIDED BY THAT
LIGHT FOR ALL OUR DAYS.

Kamala Harris

IF YOU ARE HAPPY IN YOUR OWN SKIN, IF YOU TRULY LOVE YOURSELF, THEN YOU WILL LOVE OTHER PEOPLE, AND YOU WILL BE KIND TO OTHER PEOPLE. AND THAT'S WHAT'S IMPORTANT.

Millie Bobby Brown

I'VE BEEN SEARCHING FOR WAYS TO HEAL MYSELF, AND I'VE FOUND THAT KINDNESS IS THE BEST WAY.

Lady Gaga

BE KIND WHENEVER POSSIBLE. IT IS ALWAYS POSSIBLE.

FORGET INJURIES, NEVER FORGET KINDNESSES.

Confucius

THE KINDEST THING SOMEONE HAS EVER DONE FOR ME IS BELIEVE IN ME.

Olivia Wilde

I FUNDAMENTALLY BELIEVE THIS – AND THE RESEARCH SHOWS – KINDNESS BEGETS KINDNESS.

Chelsea Clinton

IT IS IN GIVING THAT WE RECEIVE.

Francis of Assisi

WHO, IN YOUR LIFE, DO YOU REMEMBER MOST FONDLY, WITH THE MOST UNDENIABLE FEELINGS OF WARMTH? THOSE WHO WERE KINDEST TO YOU, I BET.

George Saunders

THE SMALLEST ACT
OF KINDNESS IS WORTH
MORE THAN THE
GREATEST INTENTION.

Kahlil Gibran

EVERYONE KNOWS THAT ACTS OF KINDNESS MAKE US STRONGER AND CREATE A TRUE SENSE OF COMMUNITY.

Jennifer Garner

KINDNESS CAN BE ANYTHING – FROM WATERING A TREE TO FEEDING A STRAY ANIMAL.

Jyoti Arora

CLEAR IS KIND. UNCLEAR IS UNKIND. STOP AVOIDING THE TOUGH CONVERSATIONS BECAUSE YOU THINK YOU'RE BEING POLITE OR KIND TO PEOPLE. THAT'S NOT KIND.

Brené Brown

KINDNESS IS ALWAYS IN STOCK.

Katy Perry

THAT BEST
PORTION OF
A GOOD MAN'S
LIFE, HIS LITTLE,
NAMELESS,
UNREMEMBERED
ACTS OF
KINDNESS
AND OF LOVE.

William Wordsworth

EMPATHY IS THE ONLY WAY TO LIVE. KINDNESS IS THE ONLY WAY ANY OF US ARE GOING TO SURVIVE.

Bella Hadid

THIS YEAR, MY BIRTHDAY
WISH IS A CALL FOR KINDNESS.
WE CAN'T JUST HOPE FOR A
BRIGHTER DAY, WE HAVE TO
WORK FOR A BRIGHTER DAY.

Dolly Parton

GUARD WITHIN YOURSELF
THAT TREASURE, KINDNESS.
KNOW HOW TO GIVE WITHOUT
HESITATION, HOW TO LOSE
WITHOUT REGRET, HOW TO
ACQUIRE WITHOUT MEANNESS.

George Sand

KINDNESS IS THE GOLDEN CHAIN BY WHICH SOCIETY IS BOUND TOGETHER.

Johann Wolfgang von Goethe

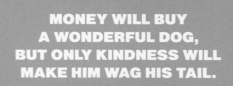

MONEY WILL BUY
A WONDERFUL DOG,
BUT ONLY KINDNESS WILL
MAKE HIM WAG HIS TAIL.

WHAT I'M ASKING YOU TODAY… DO AN ACT OF KINDNESS A DAY FOR YOU. YOU JUST MIGHT HELP SOCIETY AROUND THE WORLD.

Mark Kelly

I THINK PROBABLY KINDNESS IS MY NUMBER ONE ATTRIBUTE IN A HUMAN BEING. I'LL PUT IT BEFORE ANY OF THE THINGS LIKE COURAGE OR BRAVERY OR GENEROSITY OR ANYTHING ELSE.

Roald Dahl

**THE CHEAPEST OF ALL
THINGS IS KINDNESS,
ITS EXERCISE REQUIRING
THE LEAST POSSIBLE TROUBLE
AND SELF-SACRIFICE.**

Samuel Smiles

NEVER LOSE A CHANCE OF SAYING A KIND WORD.

William Makepeace Thackeray

I EXPECT TO
PASS THROUGH
THIS WORLD
BUT ONCE.
IF, THEREFORE,
THERE BE ANY
KINDNESS
I CAN SHOW ...

OR ANY GOOD THING THAT I CAN DO TO ANY FELLOW HUMAN BEING, LET ME DO IT NOW.

LIFE'S MOST PERSISTENT AND URGENT QUESTION IS, WHAT ARE YOU DOING FOR OTHERS?

Dr Martin Luther King Jr.

**YOU KNOW WHAT
FILLS YOU UP THE MORE
YOU KEEP GIVING IT OUT?
KINDNESS.**

Storm Reid

KINDNESS IS ALWAYS FASHIONABLE, AND ALWAYS WELCOME.

Amelia Barr

ONE OF THE DEEP SECRETS OF LIFE IS THAT ALL THAT IS REALLY WORTH DOING IS WHAT WE DO FOR OTHERS.

Lewis Carroll

GO TO WHERE YOU ARE KINDEST.

Jaron Lanier

PEOPLE HAVE SUCH KINDNESS. EVERYONE NEEDS TO KNOW THEY'RE LOVED. THERE IS ALWAYS SOMEONE OUT THERE WHO CARES ABOUT YOU, JUST REACH OUT.

Nicola Coughlan

**BE KIND TO YOURSELF
AS YOU GROW AND ALLOW
FORGIVENESS AS YOU FAIL.**

Sydney Sweeney

WHAT WISDOM CAN YOU FIND THAT IS GREATER THAN KINDNESS?

Jean-Jacques Rousseau

A PART OF KINDNESS CONSISTS IN LOVING PEOPLE MORE THAN THEY DESERVE.

Joseph Joubert

**NO ONE IS USELESS
IN THIS WORLD
WHO LIGHTENS THE
BURDENS OF ANOTHER.**

Charles Dickens

KIND HEARTS ARE THE GARDENS, KIND THOUGHTS ARE THE ROOTS, KIND WORDS ARE THE BLOSSOMS, KIND DEEDS ARE THE FRUITS.

Henry Wadsworth Longfellow

KINDNESS IS LOVE IN ACTION.

Henry Drummond

**KINDNESS
GIVES BIRTH
TO KINDNESS.**

Sophocles

BE KIND, BE PATIENT, HELP OTHERS.

Isabel Allende

Quadrille, Penguin Random House UK,
One Embassy Gardens, 8 Viaduct
Gardens, London SW11 7BW

Quadrille Publishing Limited
is part of the Penguin Random House
group of companies whose
addresses can be found at
global.penguinrandomhouse.com

Penguin
Random House
UK

Published by Quadrille in 2025

www.penguin.co.uk

A CIP catalogue record for this book
is available from the British Library

ISBN 9781784887865
10 9 8 7 6 5 4 3 2 1

Publishing Director: Kajal Mistry
Senior Commissioning Editor:
Kate Burkett
Text curated by: Satu Fox
Editorial Assistant: Harriet Thornley
Design: Claire Warner Studio
Senior Production Controller:
Sabeena Atchia

Colour reproduction by p2d

Printed in China by RR Donnelley Asia
Printing Solution Limited

The authorised representative in
the EEA is Penguin Random House
Ireland, Morrison Chambers,
32 Nassau Street, Dublin D02 YH68.

MIX
Paper | Supporting
responsible forestry
FSC® C018179
www.fsc.org